ORGANIZATIONS THAT HELP THE WORLD

AMNESTY INTERNATIONAL

MARSHA BRONSON

OTHER TITLES IN THE SERIES

Picture Credits:
Amnesty International; Chaisson Maison; Alexis Duclos; Gamma Presse; Hulton
Deutsche Collection; Mogens Norgens; Popperfoto; Rex Features; Samfoto; Frank
Spooner; Howard Zehr.

Published in Great Britain in 1992
by Exley Publications Ltd,
16 Chalk Hill, Watford,
Herts WD1 4BN, United Kingdom.

**A copy of the CIP data is available from
the British Library on request.**

ISBN 1-85015-307-8

Series editor: Helen Exley
Editor: Samantha Armstrong
Typeset by Delta, Watford
Printed at Oriental Press, UAE.

AMNESTY
INTERNATIONAL

MARSHA BRONSON

He ain't heavy, he's my brother

Guatemala City, March 4, 1990. It's a hot night. Through the city, thousands of children are looking for food on rubbish heaps, sleeping under parked cars, sitting on street corners. They are Guatemala's street kids. One of these is Nahamán Carmona López. He's thirteen years old, and he and his friends are sniffing glue on a street corner.

Suddenly, the boys are attacked by four police officers. Most of the kids manage to get away, but Nahamán is not so lucky. His friends can hear him screaming, but they are too scared to stay behind and help him. The police officers have him down on the ground and they are kicking him. When the boys finally pluck up the courage to return to the street corner, they find Nahamán unconscious, with terrible injuries. Somehow they get him to hospital, where he is found to have two broken

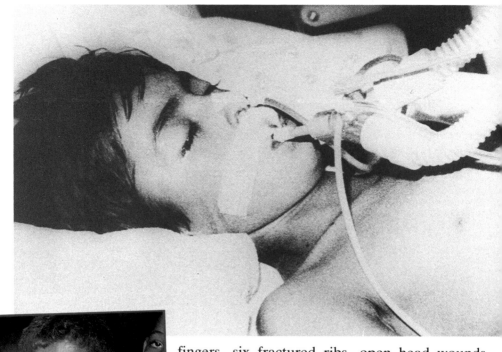

Top: Nahamán Carmona López lies unconscious in hospital, having been beaten by Guatemalan police. He later died from his injuries.
Above: These kids have no power to fight back, but Amnesty can, politely and peacefully.

fingers, six fractured ribs, open head wounds, bruising on 70% of his body and a damaged liver. He never regained consciousness.

Ten days later, the same boys gather on the streets with over a hundred other street kids. They set out to walk the two dusty miles to the Casa Alianza plot to bury Nahamán. The boy's brother helps his friends to carry the coffin. It isn't very heavy.

Since then, two of Nahamán's friends have been beaten up by the police. In a city where more than five thousand children between the ages of five and eighteen are homeless, their plight could easily go unnoticed. That is, if it were not for Amnesty International.

Amnesty heard Nahamán's story and publicized it widely. It was covered in its youth magazine, *New Release,* with vivid pictures of Nahamán healthy and smiling, and then lying with terrible injuries in his hospital bed. One picture showed the boys carrying his coffin.

Amnesty appealed for a full enquiry into his death. In response, the Guatemalan Presidential

Advisory Commission on Human Rights issued a statement saying that court proceedings had been started against four police officers in connection with the incident. But investigations proceeded much too slowly for Amnesty's liking and it became concerned that Nahamán's friends were being beaten and harassed by the police, and that witnesses of these beatings were in danger.

Amnesty got together a full report, called "Guatemala: Extrajudicial Executions and Other Human Rights Abuses Against Street Children" and distributed it everywhere it could. In October 1990, Amnesty sent a delegation to Guatemala. The delegates asked the candidates in the November presidential elections to make public the steps they proposed to take to improve human rights in Guatemala. They also made further inquiries into Nahamán's case, and discovered there was both good and bad news. In March 1991, the four police officers were sentenced to prison terms of between ten and fifteen years. However on July 19, 1991 the sentences were overturned on technical grounds. The case was re-opened, but at least two witnesses were intimidated and one was in exile.

Although the harassment and killing goes on, in this one case, Amnesty's concern paid off and those guilty were brought to justice.

Amnesty International is a worldwide organization, which was founded in 1961 by the lawyer Peter Benenson, to fight injustice. Within Amnesty there are no boundaries of politics, nationality or culture. It strives to help people in all corners of the world, and its name is known in more than 160 countries.

A new puppet show

When Amnesty began, over thirty years ago, it was intended as "a brief publicity effort". However, within one year it was an international organization with branches in seven countries.

Amnesty describes itself as a worldwide, non-political, voluntary organization which was founded "to bring relief to individual victims of injustice". It doesn't try to bring about huge changes at once. Instead it concentrates on the "individual victims". Thousands of Amnesty volunteers "twin" themselves with a prisoner somewhere in the world. In this way one person can help to free someone whom they have never met.

Most importantly, Amnesty vehemently insists that it is independent and impartial. Not everyone believes this claim to impartiality. To some it seems that such a powerful organization must be making some political statement, or backing some party. When Amnesty first started, an Iranian newspaper dismissed it as "a new puppet show that the communists have started." This was plainly untrue. Amnesty treasures its independence as its strength because it means that it does not have to hold with any government's ideology, or act according to any political leader's beliefs. It doesn't have to accept the decision of any court. Its laws are the laws of human justice.

Who is Amnesty?

Amnesty is a large group of people, each person acting on their own conviction that evil is being done in the world and that they can change it by acting together. Just how large Amnesty has become amazes even its greatest supporters. There are now over one million members in more than 160 countries. It is the world's largest voluntary organization working for human rights. There are groups of members as far apart as Moscow, Malaysia and Macau.

Amnesty has three main aims: the immediate release of all prisoners of conscience, fair and prompt trials for all political prisoners and the prevention of torture and executions. It achieves these goals by the simple method of applying pressure to governments and authorities who are behaving unjustly.

Perhaps the easiest way to appreciate the phenomenon that is Amnesty is to look at the story of how it all started.

The seed

Every huge tree grows from a small seed. The seed of Amnesty was planted in 1960. A British lawyer, Peter Benenson, read in a newspaper on the way to work one day that two Portuguese

Above: Coming from the people of Chile, graffiti says "No to Torture". Amnesty goes one step further by writing directly to the officials.

students had been arrested. A common enough occurrence, but when Benenson read further, he could hardly believe his eyes: the students had been arrested and sentenced to seven years in prison. Why? For drinking a toast to freedom in a restaurant.

The story touched a very deep chord in the lawyer. He was already painfully aware of the injustice that went on around the world. He had witnessed political trials in places as diverse as Cyprus, South Africa and Hungary. Everywhere he had seen the same miscarriages of justice and it sickened him.

He imagined setting up a campaign that would last just one year. He would call the campaign "Appeal for Amnesty, 1961" and it would be for all the prisoners who were in prison because of their religious beliefs, their political views, their sex, their race. Benenson thought of these people as "prisoners of conscience".

He wanted to help those imprisoned without fair trial and those who faced the death penalty. Suddenly, the two Portuguese students seemed to stand for all these poor, forgotten prisoners. Well, they would not be forgotten any longer. In a year it is possible to achieve a great deal.

The meeting in the café

Peter Benenson met his friend Eric Baker and together they discussed the idea excitedly. Then on Sunday, May 28, 1961, Benenson had an article published in *The Observer* newspaper that was to set the whole movement going. It was called "The Forgotten Prisoners" and on the same day there was a similar article in the French newspaper, *Le Monde*. "Appeal for Amnesty, 1961" was launched.

Benenson's offices in Mitre Court, in the heart of London, became the campaign headquarters – there was a desk and a filing cabinet. In a bar, he and Eric Baker scribbled out on paper napkins the three main aims behind the appeal that were to become its mandate, and underlie everything it stands for. And as a symbol of Amnesty's struggle

to keep the light of hope shining in a world of injustice, Peter Benenson chose a burning candle surrounded by barbed wire.

On August 3, Benenson applied to register the appeal as an official organization. "Appeal for Amnesty" gathered force with great speed and strength. Just eight weeks after *The Observer* article appeared, a Luxembourg café hosted a special meeting. There were people from Belgium, France, Ireland, Switzerland, the UK and the USA. At this meeting, what had started as a year-long appeal became a permanent movement.

Benenson's modest idea began to snowball into a highly-ambitious vision. He pictured a central library containing information on prisoners of conscience everywhere when all Amnesty had was sketchy information from scattered sources. A press conference was called after "The Forgotten Prisoners" was published. The principal speaker was a British Member of Parliament who spoke of Benenson's idea in glowing terms. The press was interested. With all the publicity, letters and money began to pour in. Information about prisoners also deluged the tiny office in Mitre Court. People began to hear about the astonishing organization whose aim was to free the forgotten prisoners. For friends and relatives or anyone who knew a prisoner of conscience, the news brought unexpected hope. They wanted to give Amnesty their full support.

The first five years

By the end of 1961 alone, after only one year's existence, there were already eleven Amnesty groups, as far apart as Norway and Australia. By February 1963 there were 180. In 1962, Amnesty took up 210 cases.

These early groups worked on three cases each: a prisoner from the East, the West and one from an Afro-Asian country. And their success rate was really encouraging. One of the prisoners mentioned in the original *Observer* article was former Archbishop of Prague, Josef Beran. In 1964, he lit a candle to celebrate his own freedom and to offer hope for the release of others. By 1966, Amnesty was exerting a great deal of pressure.

Not everyone was happy with Amnesty, however. As it became more well known, there were plenty of people who criticized it. A report on detainees in Northern Ireland claimed that they were being ill-treated. This caused great anger and condemnation of Amnesty, ironically, for pointing the finger at its country of origin. Some people simply ridiculed the organization. A 1988 report recalled that, in 1969 "the idea that ordinary people could help set free or save from torture and death men and women they had never met, in countries not their own, by writing polite letters to the government . . . was described as one of the larger lunacies of our time." But it worked and the movement grew quickly. The case histories continued to pour in.

The library of the International Secretariat in London provides vital information about injustice and previous human rights violations. Here, most of Amnesty's research is carried out by individual members of the research team. Workers sift through reports, case histories and letters.

"Work brings Freedom"... these words greeted the victims of Nazism in World War II, as they were herded into concentration camps. The camps brought death to six million Jewish people who were gassed. This scene was part of a slide show about political killings by governments, shown to the Dutch Section of Amnesty International in 1983.

"Every paragraph is a call to action, every line a condemnation of apathy, every sentence a repudiation of some moment of our individual or national history...."

UNESCO discussion about the UN Declaration of Human Rights.

Just as every tree needs a seed to grow from, it also needs the right conditions to nourish it. Although Peter Benenson's article was the action that started off Amnesty, the world must have been in a state that made such a human rights movement necessary. In another time, perhaps his plea for the forgotten prisoners would have fallen on deaf ears. Since the early years of the twentieth century, however, the world has been waking up to ideas that had never been formally recognized before.

A new consciousness has been developing: the awareness of human rights.

The Declaration of Human Rights

There has always been injustice and it has been opposed by courageous individuals and groups through the ages. But it is only in this century that basic human rights have been set down on paper. In this way, the fight for justice has become more organized and better co-ordinated. On December 10, 1948, for the first time in history, the United Nations declared that every human being has "inalienable rights". Before 1948, international law only governed matters between states, and there were no international laws for the individual. The United Nations' Declaration of Human Rights was in fact a completely revolutionary step in international law.

The United Nations published a small pamphlet called the "Universal Declaration of Human Rights". It asked all the member states to publicize the text, especially in schools and other places of education. Everyone must hear about their rights, regardless of where they lived or who governed them.

The Declaration sets out human rights in parts, called Articles: the right of freedom of expression, conscience, religion, freedom to associate with whoever you want, to assemble a group, to move about and leave your own country if you wish. It established once and for all that human rights are

extremely precious and that, at last, governments were willing to formally define them. It was a step that paved the way for the birth of Amnesty just thirteen years later.

The tree

The organization that has emerged from the seed is now extremely well-structured. At the top is the International Executive Committee – nine people from different countries who meet four times a year to carry out Amnesty's policies. These nine are elected at a meeting of the true government of Amnesty, the International Council. The Council is made up of between two and three hundred delegates, and they make all the financial decisions and changes to the statute. Then, there are "sections", and one representative from these makes up the Council. Finally, the most basic unit is the "group", which usually has between ten and fifteen members. Holding the movement together is the International Secretariat in London.

Sections can be any size. Some are extremely

The inmates of Auschwitz, one of the concentration camps, survived the worst conditions imaginable. Men, women and children were picked out at roll call for wearing glasses or for scratches on their bodies – for no reason at all – and were sent to the gas chambers. The discovery of such camps after the war helped persuade governments of the need to agree on a human rights charter. Evil on such a scale had never been seen before and, with Amnesty International in existence, will never be seen again.

large and powerful, with permanently-employed staff, several hundred groups, and several thousand members. Some sections are very small. The important thing about sections is that they co-ordinate the activities of all the members in that country. They are in direct contact with the International Secretariat and receive news and requests for action from Amnesty headquarters. They send a delegate to attend the International Council, which meets every two years. Each time the Council meets, it is at the invitation of a section in a different country.

Individuals and groups are the key to Amnesty's strength in numbers. Sections are the key to its overall unity. When you join Amnesty, you join your local group. Or, if there isn't one nearby, you can form one. Or you can just join your country's section. People from over 160 countries carry out Amnesty's work this way.

The simplest gesture

As an individual it is easy to feel helpless in the face of all the killings, imprisonment and torture. But Amnesty says that the only way to fight these feelings of helplessness is to act. And there is a very simple action that is the key to much of what Amnesty achieves: writing a letter.

This simplest of gestures, sitting down with a blank sheet of paper and a pen, has moved more mountains than would be thought possible. Amnesty has relied on the idea since the beginning with Benenson's letter to *The Observer*.

Dear Prime Minister

Imagine one afternoon you read of a letter campaign. All the details are there, who to write to, who the prisoner is and perhaps some details about their situation. You pen your letter and seal the envelope, "Dear Prime Minister.... In the post the next day your letter joins several others — "We have heard that an engineer by the name of Ghassan Najjar has been detained now in your country for many years ..." At the sorting office are more letters — "Ghassan was detained after he took part in a one-day strike to protest against the state of emergency...."

That afternoon, a plane takes off for Ghassan's native country. On board, yet more letters — "We believe that Ghassan is very ill...." Planes arrive in Ghassan's country from various destinations. On every plane, more letters — "His psychological state has been reported as very poor. Ghassan has been in prison now for eleven years, all because of one day's peaceful strike ..." In the sorting office, thousands of letters are all bound for one place — "We are most concerned about the plight of Ghassan Najjar...."

* United Nations Declaration of Human Rights Article 9: No one shall be subjected to arbitrary arrest, detention or exile.

At the government building, the letters are arriving at the rate of hundreds a day. Space has to be cleared to make way for the sudden deluge that has occurred since Ghassan became adopted by Amnesty. The letters all carry the same message — "Ghassan's detention is in breach of Article 9 of the Universal Declaration of Human Rights...." Letter upon letter upon letter — "I urge you to release Ghassan... I appeal for the unconditional release of Ghassan... Please release Ghassan Najjar...." This puts the government under pressure to release the prisoner or at least to improve their conditions. Ghassan Najjar was released in December 1991.

The subject of many letters, Ghassan Najjar was arrested in Syria during a peaceful one-day strike against the State of Emergency there. An engineer, Najjar was detained for eleven years. When Amnesty took up his case, he was very ill, physically and psychologically. After a determined letter campaign, he was released.

Amnesty is made up of young and old from over 160 countries of the world. The release of just one prisoner, relief from torture for someone or the commuting of one death sentence make it worth every effort.

Yours sincerely

Amnesty International has long been famous for its letter-writing campaigns. It is odd to think of sitting down to write a letter, not to a friend or pen-pal, but to a president, an ambassador or royalty. Yet every day, thousands of people do just that, and Amnesty has proof that, as a means of winning freedom for prisoners of conscience, the letter has no rival. The sincerity of the people who write the letters transforms a small gesture into a message of great power.

A lawyer in Peru, Carlos Escobar Pineda, tells "when I was in charge of investigating disappearances I

would be obliged by my superiors to investigate any case if we received even a single letter from Amnesty supporters about the case."

Every letter that makes its way to its destination increases the chance of a prisoner being freed. Usually, the person who sends the letter has no way of telling whether it arrived or had any effect. In most cases, letters are sent to governments or officials, who are hardly likely to have the time or

A secretary at "The Herald" in Zimbabwe receives letters from all over the world appealing against the death sentence passed against Orton and Vera Chirwa in Malawi. The abolition of the death sentence is part of Amnesty's mandate.

wish to write back. It is very rare that letters are written directly to the prisoner. Often it is not known exactly where the prisoner is. Even when it is known, Amnesty sometimes discourages writing to individuals, in case it endangers them to receive mail from an international organization.

However, occasionally a message gets back. An answer crosses the world, such as this letter from a German named H. Friedrich Muller. It was written in 1965: "Dear Miss Fitzgerald, I thank you very much for your Christmas greetings. But I didn't receive your card in jail because I was released a few weeks ago. That's too the reason that I can give you thanks. You can't imagine what a joy it has been for me to get so many greetings from Ireland. It is a good feeling to know you have friends after a long time of loneliness. As I don't know the reason for my early release (I was sent to eight years jail and I have spent only fifty months there) it is possible that Irish activity was the cause. So I'm deeply in your debt. With the best wishes for 1965, Sincerely yours, H. Friedrich Muller."

The power of the letter

Sometimes answers come from prisoners who have not been freed yet. "It's good to know I'm not fighting alone," wrote a Uruguyan prisoner to a woman who had written to her from Oklahoma, USA, "and I thank you and thank the Lord, for as long as there's persons like you, this crazy world will have hope, and people like me will have a chance to have justice done."

Even in cases where letters haven't achieved release, they can make a big difference to prisoners' situations. For example, their conditions improve, more food is allowed, torture ceases. Once the first letter bearing a foreign stamp and mentioning Amnesty arrives, those at fault know their misdeeds have been revealed. It is amazing what a powerful effect this can have.

Amnesty has strict rules about how letters should be written. The idea is not to vent feelings

of anger and outrage, but to influence the captors with reason and integrity. The letters should not be more than a page long. It helps to mention the name of a prisoner and any facts that are known. But Amnesty warns that a name should only be used if it is safe to do so and it provides recommendations about this with each prisoner's details.

The message should always be that the writer is concerned about a breach of human rights and hopes the matter will be dealt with immediately. The more personal a letter is, the better. And, says Amnesty, politeness always makes a much stronger impression than anger.

When the photographs of actual cases are too shocking, Amnesty often turns to the use of posters for their campaigns and concert publicity. Here, the mandate against torture is vividly illustrated with the Amnesty logo firmly fixed in the corner of the picture.

Tomorrow is too late!

Letters inevitably take several days to reach their destination. Postcards may take a couple of weeks. Sometimes there just isn't that time to spare. If Amnesty receives a report that a prisoner has been threatened with torture, letters may arrive too late to be of any help. Action must be taken immediately. To deal with this situation,

Amnesty has developed a technique it calls Urgent Action. Information is sent directly by telephone or telegram to urgent action committees in different countries. They, in turn, notify volunteers immediately and the volunteers send their urgent appeal by the quickest means possible: fax, telex or computer mail.

The following is an extract from the urgent action appeal that was sent out by Amnesty on October 13, 1981. The call to action urged their volunteers to remain calm. Everything must be done quickly but coolly. This particular urgent appeal was for Kapokela Sango of Zaire because he had been held without charge for twenty days.

"Recommended Action: Telegrams/Express letters in French if possible, otherwise in English (or Dutch) asking for an urgent assurance that Citoyen Kapokela Sango is being treated in accordance with internationally recognized standards and that he has not been subjected to ill-treatment. Also inquire why he was arrested, whether he has been charged and where he is held."

The urgent action appeal was headed "Fear of torture". For Kapokela the twenty-first day could have been too late.

At last! Freedom!

Over and over, there are demands for the release of a prisoner. Over and over, calls for a case to be reviewed, a trial to be held fairly, conditions to improve. If there are enough voices, Amnesty believes, the message will often be heard. And it is. Every day someone is released. In 1989, over a thousand "adopted" prisoners were freed, more than a third of those campaigned for. On this very day, the prison doors will swing open and light will stream in to dazzle the eyes of some prisoner long kept in darkness and alone. At last, light, the outside world and freedom!

The research department of Amnesty is responsible for finding out when a prisoner is freed, a detainee is given a fair trial or a hanging is commuted. It tells the people who were working on

Opposite: A painting by Uruguayan artist, German Cabera, depicts the plight of the prisoner. The isolation and desperate loneliness of imprisonment comes over so strongly in this picture, but if one Amnesty letter gets through, they have not been forgotten after all.

Below: In this poster for Amnesty, the light coming through the tiny window onto the blood-stained mattress symbolizes the light of hope that Amnesty offers. It has been proved that even the strongest bars can be pushed aside and the prisoner walk free.

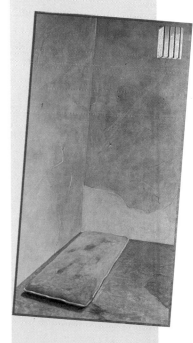

the case that it is now closed. Sometimes, it may be that torture has stopped or a political prisoner's conditions have greatly improved. Sometimes a prisoner of conscience has been set free. Whatever the case involves, Amnesty is proud of the fact that until it gets what it is campaigning for, it never gives up.

When there's good news, the research department lets everyone involved know on notepaper headed "Closure of Case". These are sweet words to read. However, what happens to the prisoner's dossier depends on the case. If the person has been set free and is not in danger of being re-arrested, the dossier, which is confidential, must be destroyed. If there is still the threat of renewed torture or a worsening of conditions, the prisoner's group keeps the dossier in a safe place.

Sometimes, there is concern about the ex-prisoner's welfare. Some people, released into the world perhaps after many years of much brutal treatment, find it very hard to cope. Amnesty doesn't let these people down. It adopted them as prisoners, now it cares for them. For at least six months after a prisoner is freed, and sometimes even longer, Amnesty members help with money, food parcels and letters of support. Aftercare, as it is called, helps an ex-prisoner remember that although the case is closed, there are still people who care.

The death sentence

Although Amnesty cares about all the rights set down in the United Nations' declaration of 1948, there are two articles in particular on which it concentrates. The first of these is Article 2, which states: "everyone has the right to life, liberty, and security of person."

In 1950, in Britain, a man named Timothy Evans was found guilty of the murder of his daughter. Sixteen years later, the main witness at that trial, John Christie, was found to have committed a series of murders himself. His testimony against Evans no longer stood up in a court of law.

The frightened face of Timothy Evans, accused in 1950 of the murder of his daughter. Sixteen years later, Evans was cleared of the crime because of unreliable evidence. It was too late: he had been hanged for the murder. Amnesty International opposes the death penalty in all cases. Although 40% of death sentences have been commuted in recent years, execution is legal in more than one hundred countries.

Evans was granted a pardon. But it was too late: his punishment in 1950 was to hang.

What good did it do, discovering this man was innocent? What good is a posthumous pardon? And Timothy Evans is not the only one. In this century, in the United States alone, no less than twenty-three people have been put to death and then later found to be innocent.

There are times when Amnesty International is faced with a very difficult decision. It has to decide whether or not to take on cases of people who themselves may have abused human rights.

But in one situation, Amnesty feels that there is no difficult decision: the death penalty. There is no going back, no rectifying mistakes, once someone has been condemned to die. Amnesty opposes this punishment – whether it is by shooting, electrocution, lethal injection, hanging, stoning or decapitation – in every case. No matter what the person has done, the death penalty denies a person their basic right to life. To Amnesty, taking away a person's life, whether as crime or punishment, is wrong.

February 23, 1985: the public execution of ten convicted armed robbers in Nigeria. Being shot while tied to a barrel is just one of the ways the death penalty is carried out. Amnesty opposes all methods of execution. The bodies are roughly taken down in front of the thousands of people who have come to watch.

Don't leave me

"When I leave, my client begs me not to go. As the guards take him back to his cell, he often starts to cry." These words were spoken in 1989 by a death row lawyer in Alabama, USA, Bryan Stevenson. His client was fifteen years old.

In the USA you are not allowed to vote or to buy alcohol until you are eighteen; but you can be sentenced to death. Between 1985 and 1991, four people between the ages of twelve and seventeen were sentenced to death in America. By July 1991, there were thirty-one people under the age of eighteen on death row in twelve American states. Amnesty International states that the death penalty must be abolished no matter who is being sentenced or what their crime is. And it believes that sending children to their death is the greatest horror of all.

Below: Various forms of execution are in use in different countries. Pictured here is the electric chair, in use in the United States. The victim is strapped into the chair and a lethal current of electricity is passed through their body by means of electrodes.

Just let me live

Dalton Prejean was seventeen in 1978. In May of that year he was convicted of murdering a white policeman. Prejean was black, but the prosecutor excluded all black people from serving on the jury. The judge also moved the trial to a white area of Louisiana. The lawyer defending Prejean had never before handled a case for which the punishment would be the death sentence. Also, he was appointed by the court and not by the accused. It was Prejean's right to appoint his own lawyer to defend him, but he was too poor to do so. He might have got a fairer trial if he had. As it was, he was convicted by an all-white jury, with only an inexperienced lawyer on his side: the sentence was death.

There were plenty of other details to do with Prejean that should have been taken into account at his trial and were not. To start with, his lawyer never mentioned to the court that Prejean had been abused and neglected as a child; or that he had a history of mental illness and had been diagnosed as a schizophrenic. When he was only fourteen, he had been convicted of another murder and at that point, doctors had recommended that he be admitted to hospital for "a long stay". They had discovered some damage in his brain that caused him to lose control of his actions when he was under stress. This evidence never emerged at the trial. Doctors saw Prejean's need for help, but the court never heard about it.

We all make mistakes

The saddest thing of all is that the one fact that could not be hidden, his youth, was not used in his defence. No one said to the judge: "But he was only seventeen! He was still a child in the eyes of the law. Won't you give him the rest of his life to change?" The boy didn't ask for anything more. "I don't ask to get out of prison," he said. "I just ask to live with my mistake.... We all make mistakes in life." Amnesty felt that the jury who sentenced him answered one mistake with another. Even when Prejean appealed against his sentence, and the facts of his illness were made known, the state governor ordered his execution. After twelve years on death row, Dalton Prejean died in the electric chair on May 18, 1990.

Who can decide?

It is too late to decide that Timothy Evans was innocent, or that Dalton Prejean really should have had medical help instead of the electric chair. In the same year as Evans was hanged, a Japanese man named Sakae Menda was also sentenced to death for murder. In 1983, he was declared innocent and set free. He was lucky – or was he? For thirty-three years he had lived on death row, in the shadow of death. Sentenced prisoners wait on death row for their sentences to be carried out.

"The gallows is not only a machine of death but a symbol. It is the symbol of terror, cruelty and irreverence for life; the common denominator of primitive savagery, medieval fanaticism and modern totalitarianism."

Arthur Koestler, Hungarian-born author.

magine what it must be like to live in the knowledge hat at any moment, those footsteps outside your cell ould be the guard coming to tell you that your time o die has come.

Amnesty believes the death penalty is wrong. Who can decide that another person should die? Amnesty's answer is: no one. And yet the death penalty is still legal in over one hundred countries ncluding South Africa, Turkey and the countries hat formerly made up the Soviet Union. Studies 1ave shown that abolition of the death penalty does 1ot lead to an increase in the rate of capital crime. Perhaps the most chilling criticism of this punishment are the words Amnesty published of executioner Albert Pierrepoint, "All the men and women I have faced at that final moment convince ne that in what I have done I have not prevented a single murder."

One organization, even one as powerful as Amnesty, can hardly hope to combat such a widespread abuse of human rights, but Amnesty finds the answer in the individual. Amnesty is made up of individuals, each on their own as powerless as the prisoners they campaign for. Behind each campaign is one face and one story. The members of Amnesty pool their strength, and that is how Amnesty's battles are won.

1+1=3...this poster very simply shows just how victims of torture are forced to say just what someone wants to hear, regardless of whether it is the truth or not. Amnesty hears of every kind of torture: from torture to extract the truth to cruel punishment for telling it.

Torture

The second Article of the UN's Declaration of Human Rights that Amnesty pays special attention to is Article 5. This states, "No one shall be subjected to torture or to cruel, inhuman or degrading treatment or punishment."

These are words that crop up again and again. They mean severe beatings on the body and the soles of the feet with rubber hoses and truncheons, electric shocks being run through the genitals and tongue, near-drownings, hanging by rms and legs, cigarette burns all over prisoners' houlders, sleep deprivation or subjecting to a igh-pitched noise. And much more. These words re repeated all through Amnesty's leaflets and ewsletters, in the organization's mandate, in rgent action appeals and in the letters members vrite – "cruel, inhuman or degrading treatment r punishment." Amnesty knows that two out of hree people on earth live in a country where tor- ure occurs. "Torture is a fundamental violation f human rights," one Amnesty leaflet declares, '... an offence to human dignity and prohibited nder national and international law."

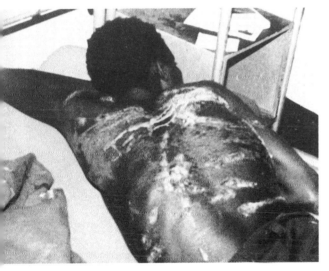

At the end of the 1970s, Amnesty published a review of the decade. In it torture was described as "an epidemic that seemed to spread like a cancer in the seventies". And in the eighties tor- ure was reported from more than ninety countries. One point Amnesty tries hard to bring home to people is that torture is not something that only happens in Third World countries. Cer- tain regions do have a notorious history of abus- ing human rights, but many countries carry out cruel, inhuman and degrading treatment of their citizens – even in some of the most "enlightened" countries like France, Italy and Britain where police ill-treatment is known to occur.

"On 10 December 1948 the United Nations General Assembly proclaimed the Universal Declaration of Human Rights without dissent. The governments of the world agreed, for the first time in history, to a statement of every person's basic human rights.... They promised to work towards a world without cruelty and injustice.

"They didn't keep the promise ... more than half of the world's governments gaol people in violation of their human rights. A third of the world's governments torture their prisoners."
John G. Healey,
Executive Director of
Amnesty International USA.

31

* United Nations Declaration of Human Rights Article 5: *No one shall be subjected to torture or to cruel, inhuman or degrading treatment or punishment.*

In October 1983, Amnesty put together a twelve point plan for the prevention of torture. It told governments how they could take steps to prevent the torture of prisoners. For example, the highest authorities of a country can make statements telling the law enforcers that torture will not be tolerated. Amnesty called for an end to secret detention and the use of statements extracted under torture. It asked governments to make torture illegal and to prosecute those found guilty of it. It suggested that places where prisoners are held be visited and examined regularly so that the public knows what goes on.

The chain of events

The information that is needed to prepare documents like these comes from many different countries. The Amnesty International tree has branches all over the world. Its roots are in London and this is where each case begins. There are several stages a case goes through. Until all the facts have been checked, an individual who

Amnesty's attention is simply under investigation. The investigation has to take place at great speed. Quick action is essential as there may be a life at stake.

Imagine then, the beginnings of a case. The details of a story are rushed to the International Secretariat in London. Case details include the prisoner's name; their nationality and what has happened to them; whether they have gone missing or their whereabouts are known; if they have been beaten or there is a threat of torture; what kind of conditions they are being kept in; whether they have been allowed to exercise their rights to a lawyer. There is a constant sense of urgency. This information may reach the International Secretariat just hours after someone is taken.

Life blood

The details of a case are dealt with by Amnesty's research department, which is the life blood of the whole organization. It is the research department that first looks into a case. To start with, it establishes certain facts: Are the prisoner's conditions below the international standards? Is the punishment going on too long? Is there mental or physical damage? All these questions need to be answered before a prisoner is eligible for "adoption".

By the early 1990s, there were forty research teams, each dealing with its own separate region of the world. But the department grew from humble beginnings. Anne Burley, head of the Europe region, joined Amnesty in 1968. "There weren't any teams or even research regions", she remembers. "In those days there was a small core of paid research staff who were responsible for a large number of countries — if you did the Soviet Union, you were also responsible for Eastern Europe *and* half of Western Europe as well!"

Today, things are much more professional. Yet it is often hard for the researchers to get hold of all the information they need. Modern communications make it easy to pass news on quickly, but

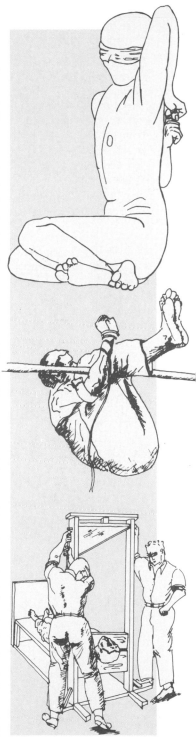

news filters through in many ways, some obvious and some unlikely. Because Amnesty has so many members worldwide, newspapers, journals and radio broadcasts are a valuable source of information. Then there are the more unusual methods news travels by.

The friendly hitchhikers

It might seem unlikely that two hitchhikers in Argentina, who were given a lift by a total stranger, would later save that man's life. Yet that is exactly what happened. A couple, hiking across Argentina, were picked up by a clerk named Pedro Rodriguez. The three became friends. Two years later, Rodriguez was imprisoned and tortured because he criticized the Argentinian military government. His hitchhiking friends heard of his plight through his family, and immediately contacted Amnesty. The wheels were put in motion to campaign for Rodriguez's release.

In fact, Rodriguez's story has a happy ending. When Amnesty was celebrating its thirtieth birthday, Pedro was there celebrating too. There were thirty scarlet and black banners, one for each year. Each showed a picture of someone whose case Amnesty had worked on during that year and Pedro Rodriguez carried his own for the year 1974. And when the time came to drink a toast of Portuguese wine to commemorate those two hitchhikers, it was Pedro who asked the marchers to raise their glasses to "Liberty!"

The professionals

As well as its trained research staff, Amnesty has a team of lawyers who examine closely the laws under which a prisoner is being detained. Lawyers are in a particularly strong position to complain on behalf of the victims of human rights abuses. They look at a country's constitution, and how its courts work. If they find the prisoner's detention is actually against the law, Amnesty's case is strengthened. Amnesty is not bound by the laws of any country. It has laws of its own: the laws of justice and of fair treatment.

But sometimes, there is reason to despair. There are clever lawyers working against good as well. In Chile, in January 1990, military courts called up an old law made in 1978. They used it to close three investigations into the disappearances of more than a hundred people.

Another group of professionals working for Amnesty includes doctors. And doctors work on both sides, too. Some assist in the torturing of prisoners. But there are ten thousand doctors working in thirty countries for Amnesty.

Publicity

To get prisoners released is often a complicated and difficult process. Perhaps one of the greatest forces Amnesty puts to work is publicity.

Governments are very concerned about their "image". No one likes to be seen committing atrocities. If all the evil can be carried out under the cover of secrecy, in the dead of night, in remote

A member of Amnesty closely examines the information that pours into the International Secretariat in London. Every day hundreds of letters and packages arrive, each one telling of a human being in distress. In 1991, Amnesty dealt with more than 2,400 cases involving over 3,300 individuals. Urgent Actions, each generating thousands of appeals to authorities, were initiated 605 times on 79 countries. Over 1,330 prisoners were released.

Argentinian writer, Jacobo Timmermann, was arrested by the military junta in 1977. A famous journalist and former owner of Buenos Aires newspaper, "La Opinion", Jacobo Timmermann's opinions were not popular with some and he became one of Amnesty's prisoners of conscience.

places, then it is easier to get away with it. A government can present a good face to the world in the light of day and no one will know the difference. Amnesty tries to turn the eyes of the world on these governments. It tries to remove the cloak of secrecy so that the world can see what is going on. It tells people to speak out, write off to the governments involved, to say, "We know what you're doing". In the glare of the world's television cameras and journalist's questions, it is hard for the culprits to shrink back into secrecy.

As *Young A.I.*, the magazine for young Amnesty members, pointed out in one issue: "Amnesty works because it embarrasses governments to have their darker deeds revealed to the world".

The world is watching

News stories travel quickly every day; someone sees a headline on a newspaper stand, someone reads an article in the paper and tells their friends about it. Bad news often travels faster than good, and everyone is interested in a story. But even when Amnesty's stories don't make the headlines, they have many different ways of passing information. Publicity is available in the form of leaflets, newsletters, posters, word of mouth, information letters, press releases, studies of countries and mission reports. Amnesty uses them all.

In 1987, a Kampuchean teenager wrote to Amnesty saying that he had read a report it had published about its campaign, launched worldwide that year, to stop torture and political imprisonment in Kampuchea. The report had been translated into Khmer and the boy found and read it in the refugee camp where he lived, on the border with Thailand.

And then there are also the less obvious forms of publicity. And Amnesty finds that these can be even more effective in catching people's attention because they are a novelty. In the streets of Lima, in Peru, members of Amnesty paraded up and down in costume. When the passers-by stopped and stared, they were told that these curiously dressed people were protesting against the death penalty in the United States.

Prisoners of conscience

However, not all cases can be taken up by Amnesty. Because it is independent and impartial it has to be very careful that its actions are not interpreted wrongly. Many more questions must be asked before Amnesty adopts a prisoner.

For example, if they were involved in violence. Amnesty does not campaign for their release, although it will still press for a fair trial and oppose torture and execution. Some people resented and questioned the strict non-violence clause in Amnesty's mandate. Surely, they pointed out, people have been compelled to react violently as a last resort against repression. It was only in 1991 that Amnesty changed its mandate to allow those who acted violently in self-defence to be considered for adoption as prisoners of conscience.

This highlights the important distinction the organization makes between prisoners of conscience and other prisoners. Amnesty opposes the death penalty and torture in all cases, no matter what the victims have done, but it only opposes the imprisonment of detainees who are prisoners of conscience.

So Amnesty must find out the reasons behind an arrest or disappearance, and then decide whether the prisoner is a prisoner of conscience or not. Then it has to make sure that none of its actions will overlap with the efforts of other organizations, like, for example, reform groups. Amnesty's powers might be more useful on another case no one has taken up.

Tough decisions

Tempting though it might seem to jump straight in and help someone who appears to be in trouble, some serious consideration must be given to further aspects of each case. Amnesty has to step back and consider its own position. What it stands

André Sakharov, a beloved figure to many Russians, spoke out strongly against the violation of human rights in the former Soviet Union. For his courage, he was sent into exile in the town of Gorky, where he remained for many years until he was invited home to Moscow when Mikhail Gorbachev was in power.

for, its mandate, must always be kept in mind.

There is a danger that, if the organization gets involved, the action might appear to be a political move. Amnesty could be seen to be looking for a bargain, for example, an exchange of prisoners. And that must never happen.

Amnesty asks for the unconditional release of prisoners of conscience. It isn't interested in deals. It won't negotiate or mediate between opposing governments. Any help given is completely free of political motive. Amnesty cannot afford to be compromised.

Amnesty also has to make sure the sources of information are trustworthy. It would be easy for someone to supply false information and then use such a powerful group for propaganda. The researchers are well aware of this danger. In the beginning, they only took on the cases of those they were absolutely convinced were prisoners of conscience. Now they base their decisions on the knowledge and experience they have gained over more than thirty years. After hundreds of stories have come in from one country, researchers can see patterns of abuse and injustice. They know what to expect: what kind of people are likely victims, how they are likely to be treated, and where they may be.

Action!

Finally, once all the facts have been checked and double-checked, Amnesty makes the decision whether to adopt the prisoner or not. Once Amnesty feels the organization is right, it *acts*. Now everyone swings into action.

First the prisoner of conscience is assigned to a specific group. This group must be in a separate country from the one where the prisoner is being detained. This is so that everyone is working for a fellow human being, not just because they come from the same place. It also helps to give the offending government a sense that the world really is watching. Information on whom to write to, lists of addresses, and facts on the case are then given to the group members to begin writing those letters.

Bigger projects

But Amnesty thinks big too. In July 1991, it urged the United Nations to set up an on-site operation in Iraq, to monitor human rights and try to prevent the tortures and killings going on there. It published a report at the same time, telling of its delegates' visits to Iraq and Turkey in May 1991. The delegates interviewed Kurds and Arab Shi'a Muslims about the uprising in March and April of that year, and reported many arrests and executions of those who had been suspected of taking part in the uprising.

Amnesty International believed that human rights violations had reached such a shocking level that it was time to call on the United Nations and ask it to ensure the protection of those in such danger in Iraq. Although Amnesty works closely with the United Nations and puts cases before the United Nations Commission on Human Rights, it had never made such an appeal for immediate action before.

Amnesty also "thinks big" by organizing

campaigns on a massive scale, designed to reach vast audiences. The 1989 campaign against the death penalty was one of these. It was designed to spread the main arguments against the penalty in sixteen of the countries where it is carried out most frequently. In twelve of the sixteen countries, local Amnesty groups managed to get letters and articles condemning the death penalty published. One of the most popular magazines in Japan, the youth magazine, *Syukan Playboy,* which is not noted for its opposition to capital punishment, published an article saying it had received many letters from Amnesty members about the use of the death penalty in Japan.

The delegates in the gallery

After a group has been given the prisoner's details, duties are assigned to the people who will work in other ways to help secure a release. For example, there may be a delegation sent to observe a trial. This is not always a successful mission. In 1983, Amnesty delegates were refused access to the trial of Orton Chirwa and his wife Vera in Malawi. There is no knowing how much a couple of Amnesty delegates at that trial might have helped ensure justice was done. But the Malawi government wasn't taking any risks. Amnesty was banned from the courtroom and there was nothing it could do about it.

It is certain that having delegates sit in on trials has made a difference in the past. Amnesty members carry with them a sense of power in this situation. Governments look guilty if they prevent impartial bystanders from observing what goes on. Out of fear, the courts will often let Amnesty delegates in when ordinary members of the public are not allowed. Amnesty knows that secret trials are often rigged. But few countries would be willing to alter evidence in front of the world.

As well as attending trials, Amnesty delegates visit embassies, draw up petitions, lobby politicians and try to persuade journalists to take up the prisoners' stories. It is often the quiet work

A prisoner is led away by armed guards in Chile. Thousands of people have gone missing in Chile and mass graves have been discovered, containing dozens of unidentified bodies. People were taken away in the middle of the night and never seen again. Those who were left behind could only wonder what kind of treatment their relatives would suffer.

* United Nations Declaration of Human Rights Article 3: *Everyone has the right to life, liberty and security of person.*

DESDE CHILE... UN ABRAZO A LA ESPERANZA
CONCIERTOS AMNESTY INTERNATIONAL
ESTADIO NACIONAL   12 Y 13 - OCTUBRE '90

that goes on in the background that gets results or a word in the ear of a government official that prompts the case to be brought up in parliament. Or maybe somebody, somewhere, seeing a small article in a news paper will be in a position to help.

New problems

Over the years, Amnesty's methods of working on cases have changed with the nature of the cases themselves. In the late 1970s, for example, there seemed to be less information available about prisoners. Amnesty knew there were still as many as before, but governments were becoming more subtle. More people were simply disappearing without trace. Instead of improving human rights, governments were just closing down channels of communication – refusing to grant visas to Amnesty observers, refusing access to journalists and withholding information about missing people, even from their relatives.

The Embrace of Hope: Thousands gathered between October 12 and 13, 1990 in Santiago's Olympic Stadium for concerts to publicize the plight of Chile's "disappeared". This press conference told the world why the concerts were needed and why Amnesty needs as many people's support as possible.

41

There was non-violent repression that still affected people deeply and that Amnesty strongly opposed. In Bulgaria, Turkish minorities were being forced to take Bulgarian names and all traces of Turkish culture and language were being suppressed.

By the end of the 1980s, however, there were several more "modern" violations of human rights becoming widespread. Hostage-taking was one. Imprisoning completely sane political opponents in psychiatric hospitals was another. And there was the increasing problem of refugees. Amnesty became very concerned about the fifty thousand Vietnamese people that were being held in Hong Kong, having come there by every means possible looking for asylum.

Most of these people were waiting to be "screened" – a process which decides whether they are considered refugees or not. Those who are "screened out" or denied refugee status risk being returned to Vietnam. But obviously, fearing imprisonment and ill-treatment if they are sent back, many refugees will do anything rather than return. If they refuse to go back, they could be detained in Hong Kong in appalling camp conditions or physically forced to return to the hell they fled.

To combat this clampdown on information, Amnesty began to launch "theme" publicity campaigns to help people focus on the emerging problems. In October 1983, there was the "Murder by Governments" campaign. Then there was "Columbia: stop the death squads", and "Disappearance in Sri Lanka".

Nobel Peace Prize

On its tenth birthday in 1971 Amnesty received one of the highest awards in the world: the Nobel Peace Prize. And in 1972 its work was again recognized publicly when it was awarded the United Nations Human Rights Prize.

These prizes helped greatly to bring Amnesty to the attention of the public and people flocked to join. In the mid-1980s, one year alone saw a 30% rise in membership. At the end of 1985, there were 250,000 members, at the end of 1986 there were 350,000. By 1992, there were more than one million members and Amnesty had become the world's largest humanitarian organization.

Who pays the bills?

An organization as large as this needs a large bank balance to match. Although most people give Amnesty their time and skills for nothing, things have changed a lot from the few unpaid workers of the early days. In 1991, Amnesty's budget was the equivalent of seventeen million American dollars.

The money comes from membership and fund-raising. In the beginning, the organization sometimes found fund-raising difficult: people were so enthusiastic about fighting for human rights that

Opposite top: For years Vietnamese boat people, who poured into Hong Kong in their thousands to escape human rights repression in their own country, found themselves living in detention camps, sometimes in intolerable conditions. At the Whitehead Detention Center, they form a human message of despair, sending out an S.O.S. to the free world. Opposite below: A Vietnamese family arrives in Hong Kong. Most await "screening" to determine whether they will be granted refugee status, or forcibly returned to Vietnam. Amnesty seeks improvements in this screening process.

Above: Amnesty organizes some fun! Despite being crammed against the barriers and the heat, these rock fans are clearly having a good time. Amnesty International, because of its important work, attracts big names, especially in the rock world. The concerts then work for both parties – the fans enjoy the music and awareness of the organization is raised.

they often overlooked the need for money. But to be effective, Amnesty must be realistic. Awareness of the need for funds has grown over the years. While one 1964 newsletter complained that groups weren't sending in their yearly subscriptions, groups today often send in over ten times the subscriptions of their total membership.

No limits

There is no limit to the way people can raise money. There are the popular sponsored walks, cycles and swims; cake and garage sales,

Above: Amnesty workers in Oslo publicize the right for justice. It is important for people to know their rights so that they can make sure they are being upheld. Amnesty's work encourages people to oppose torture, abolish the death penalty and to fight for the release of prisoners of conscience. The organization is growing all the time.

* An effective and popular movement of well-meaning, stubborn people who will not go away or shut-up – backed by impartial authoritative research.

Description of Amnesty
in 1983 Handbook.

Christmas cards, raffles and concerts. But more exciting ways of earning are continually being invented. One man held a pot-throwing contest. There have been sponsored jailbreaks, where people dressed in the exaggerated stripes of prison garb leave a certain spot with a small amount of money, and have to make it to a chosen destination as fast as they can only using that sum. Sometimes they carry chains and handcuffs to publicize the break. It's done in a spirit of fun, in spite of the sobering reason for it all.

In Peru in 1990, Amnesty organized workshops for teenagers living in the shanty towns around

Lima. There was an arts workshop, too, and at the end of the year, Amnesty in Lima published a booklet of poems written by the eleven to fourteen year olds who took part in the workshop. It was called *Derechos Humanos, Una Esperanza* ("Human Rights – The Hope") and the poems, like the one below, were all on the theme of life and liberty.

SPANISH VERSION	ENGLISH TRANSLATION
Ojala el mundo sea un paraiso con estrellas de paz y alegria,	Oh that the world were a paradise with stars of peace and happiness
juntus seamos un borrador para borrar lo malo que hemos escrito.	Together let's be an eraser to rub out all that we've written.
Que suelten a la paloma de la Paz para que vuele por los cielos de la libertad.	Then let's free the dove of peace so that it can fly in the heavens of freedom.
Ojala el mundo sea un paraiso para que brinde el amor	Oh the the world can be a paradise We can have love
sin tantos i stmos que creen abismos.	Without anything that makes us sad.
Si todos nos damos las manos todo puede ser posible.	If we all hold hands Everything is possible.
(Creacion colectiva)	(Collective creation)

The grandmother's story

Opposite: The mothers and grandmothers of the Argentinian "disappeared" mark the sixth anniversary of their weekly protest marches. The group, known as "Madres de Plaza de Mayo," was formed in 1977 to demand information about lost relatives. Amnesty has been helping them in their search ever since.

In certain countries, like Argentina and Chile, men and women are arrested for no apparent reason and the authorities then refuse to acknowledge any responsibility or to disclose their whereabouts. In Argentina, over a seven year period, more than fifteen thousand people went missing in this way. Many were secretly executed without ever being charged with a crime. Often, when mothers and fathers are missing or are killed, their children disappear. Pregnant women are abducted and no one ever knows what becomes of their babies. Or the children are taken in by the families of prison guards and officials.

Ramon Camps, a senior military figure in Argentina, once spoke out about this: "Personally I did not eliminate any child," he said. "What I did was to take some of them to charitable organizations so that they could find new parents."

But with their parents gone, it is left to the

NIÑOS DESAPARECIDOS
PLAZA de MAYO
PARICIO
IDOS - D
PLAZA DE
PARI

The grandmothers of Plaza de Mayo, "Abuelas de Plaza de Mayo" refuse to be intimidated into silence in their search for missing children and grandchildren. Here they march in the streets of Buenos Aires to show their unity and resistance to the Argentinean government. The National Commission on Disappeared People documented 8,960 cases of "disappearance" during the military juntas' rule from 1976 to 1983.

grandparents to look for these children. In 1977, the Argentinian grandmothers united in a group, with the support of Amnesty, called *Abuelas de Plaza del Mayo*. They set to work on a seemingly impossible task.

When a parent wants to prove a child is theirs, they can get blood tests done. If the blood tests match in a certain way, the child can be positively proved to be theirs. With grandparents, a generation again removed, these tests have to be a lot more complicated. But they can be done. A special genetic test has been developed. Doctors can say what percentage of likelihood there is that a relationship exists. As the Amnesty *Journal* stated, "Science is a search for knowledge, a search for truth. Today in Argentina it has also become a search for justice."

By 1987, the science was so far advanced, and the movement so strong that a Genetic Data Bank was set up in Argentina. Genetic information was stored there in case grandparents should die

while the search for the children was still underway. Relatives of missing children are allowed to have free blood tests done to check for matches. So far, more than two hundred disappeared children have been searched for and fifty have been located. Forty-three of these were still living, with new parents.

One of these success stories began on April 2, 1976 when an Argentinian woman, Graciela Artés, was arrested in La Paz, Bolivia. With her was her nine-month-old daughter, Carla. Graciela was kept in the Ministry of the Interior. Carla was sent to an orphanage. There, she was registered under a false name. Then on August 29, both mother and daughter were taken over the border. Nothing was ever seen of Graciela again and the grandmother thought that both her daughter and her granddaughter were surely dead.

Then, nine years later, a man was arrested on suspicion of being a member of an Argentinian death squad. Blood tests were done on his nine-year-old adopted daughter. It was Carla. A federal judge was shown the evidence from the tests – and Carla was reunited with her grandmother.

And women must weep

Amnesty laments the fate of women who are victims in more ways than one. They too are deprived of their rights. Not only are their loved ones snatched from them, but they are denied access to them, sometimes even all information about them. If they dare to ask, they could suffer the same fate. In the Philippines, a young girl was threatened with death because she asked the authorities where her father had been taken.

Life is miserable in the shadow of those who seem to have just disappeared off the face of the earth. The women, who don't know if their family is alive or dead, continue to try to trace them. But if a woman's husband is simply missing and has not been declared dead, she may not even be allowed to draw a widow's pension.

Sometimes a woman can be persecuted as an

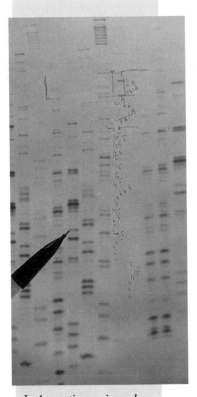

In Argentina, science has been put to work in the search for the missing, and the identification of the dead. A genetic data bank allows genetic testing that can prove the identity of kidnapped children. In 1984, a group of forensic experts formed the Argentinean Forensic Anthropology Team who have special skills in "unearthing the past".

The Grandmothers of the Disappeared at an Amnesty concert. So far they have located fifty children, at least forty-three of whom were living with new families.

Opposite: Relatives of political prisoners chain themselves to railings at the Congress in Santiago, Chile, in March 1987. They were protesting against the dealth penalty.

indirect result of husband, brothers and sons. In Syria, sixty-seven women were arrested between August 1987 and February 1988 and detained without trial until December 1991 because they were related to men who were suspected of being subversives.

Amnesty is very aware of the plight of women and constantly highlights it. The groups that women themselves form, like the Mothers of the Disappeared in Chile or a group called Comrades in El Salvador, help to get information to Amnesty about abuses to women. Amnesty's Women's Network constantly brings women's issues to the fore in campaigns.

The women in the Women's Network truly

belong to the twentieth century. They are able to fight for their rights. But Amnesty still uncovers frightening evidence that some women today might as well be living three hundred years ago. In 1987, Amnesty received information that women in Mozambique were being tried as witches and executed. In Iran, women can still be stoned for committing adultery.

The practice of freedom

Article 26 of the UN Declaration of Human Rights states: "Everyone has the right to education". Education, it says, should result in people learning about and respecting human rights. Education is a tool for understanding and liberation.

In 1983, Amnesty decided it was time to bring human rights officially into the classroom. It published its first education pack. Many teachers made use of the pack and it became standard text. It was called "Teaching and Learning about Human Rights". In 1991, Amnesty brought out its second education pack. This one was called

Amnesty unlocks the door of cruelty and injustice by non-violent protests. The letter campaigns, marches and visits of delegations prove much more successful than violence.

"Working for Freedom", and it included units about writers whose works had been banned and the "disappeared" of Latin America.

The schoolchildren of Norway really put that "working for freedom" idea into practice. One day every year, they leave their desks, go out on the streets and get to work in any way they can think of. By the 1990s over a quarter of a million schoolchildren were taking part. Some of them make and sell home-made cakes on street corners. Some wash cars or shine shoes. They will tidy attics, clean windows or mow lawns. They call the day, *Operasjon Dagsverk*, or "Operation A Day's Work". Every krone goes to a charity or cause. In 1990 Amnesty was chosen.

Spending the money

Amnesty is not secretive about how its funds are used. Not only does it publish its audited accounts every year with the annual report, but it frequently issues statements to the press and special reports about finances. The money from *Operasjon Dagsverk 1990* was sent to a human rights education project involving fifteen countries in Asia, Africa and Latin America. The organizer of the day, a nineteen-year-old student, Lars Alsaker, explained why the children felt education was such an important starting point for the spread of human rights.

"In many countries in the Third World," he said, "people don't know about their human rights. This, of course, makes it very easy to suppress them and to violate their rights. People do not claim and fight for rights they don't know they have. And only people aware of their rights will respect the rights of others."

To help spread this knowledge, Amnesty arranged for the money to be used to buy books and teaching materials that were all about human rights, and sent them to Third World countries. Now, when the children of Guntur in India are learning to read and write, they are also learning about their right to freedom of expression and

The logo designed for Amnesty's thirtieth anniversary. The simple shape of the person's head symbolizes the huge number of people who Amnesty have fought for since its conception in 1961.

* **Amnesty International relies on donations from its members and the public. It must continue to be – and be seen to be – financially independent. By far the greatest part of the movement's funds come from small individual donations, membership fees, and local fund-raising drives. These help to build a broad popular movement, backed up by financial support from the public throughout the world.**

From an Amnesty International factsheet.

The chains of torture: Amnesty receives reports of people tortured for many different reasons – religion, ethnic origins, sex and political beliefs. One out of three people live in a country where torture is carried out.

movement. By the time they can read, they already know it is wrong to discriminate against anyone because of religion or race. Their books use Indian folklore to illustrate these points.

In Brazil, more than a million young people have been learning about human rights through Amnesty slide shows and videos. In Tunisia, a library specially devoted to books on the subject is being set up, and conferences are taking place too. A generation of people is emerging with a firm grasp of the rights and the courage to fight for them. All this was made possible by the children of Norway.

Big business

Amnesty has always relied on the money from individuals and small groups. But for the first couple of decades, it somehow seemed as though the doors to the world of big business were closed to the organization. Large corporations have often protested in the past that human rights have nothing to do with them. But this is all changing.

In Holland, trainee executives sit watching a video. It's a film of the top five executives in the country. In the film, a kidnapping takes place – one of the members of staff goes missing. It's not real, only a staged replay based on the facts of an Amnesty case. The executives discuss the case, human rights and what kind of role big companies can play in promoting them. They talk about company ethics, how business should respond in situations where they might be helping terrorism or torture by their actions. All five of the executives in the video are members of Amnesty.

The club

For more than ten years, these executive have been contacts of a successful club, known as the Amnesty Business Club – or *Al Commissie Bedrijfsleven*. All of the members of this club are, or were, senior officials in international companies, and they joined because they felt the business world is not paying enough attention to human rights. For example, companies sell equipment without checking whether it will be used for political repression.

Businesses often invest in development without finding out how this will affect the area and the people who already live there. Companies were also doing business with a country where torture and disappearances are widespread.

The Amnesty Business Club now supplies companies with information about the countries Amnesty is worried about. Pleading ignorance is no longer acceptable. Amnesty dismisses arguments that business has nothing to do with human rights or that commerce has no influence. Members of the Business Club quite often approach senior officials in big companies and tell them, usually confidentially, about prisoners in the countries they are doing business with.

Club members also take action on behalf of business people who are prisoners of conscience, or are being tortured. Kenneth Matiba, a prominent businessman in Kenya, was arrested on July 4, 1990. There were other businessmen arrested with him, and they were all campaigning for another party in Kenya because the country is not a democracy. Mr. Matiba was imprisoned in solitary confinement. He suffered from high blood pressure and had a stroke in prison because he was not allowed medical aid. His Dutch colleagues campaigned for his release and in June 1991 Mr Matiba was released and allowed to go abroad for medical treatment. Six months later the government allowed the opposition – and Mr. Matiba – to form political parties.

Advertising and sponsorship

Amnesty International is learning how to catch the attention of big business through advertising. With care, it can set up the kind of campaign that doesn't compromise its position. There is always the danger that sponsorship has a negative side and Amnesty must make sure of the motives of its

"The candle burns not for us, but for all those whom we failed to rescue from prison, who were shot on the way to prison, who were tortured, who were kidnapped, who 'disappeared'. That's what the candle is for."
Peter Benenson.

The Amnesty logo is a candle surrounded by barbed wire. The flame burns for all prisoners of conscience, unfairly imprisoned political prisoners and victims of torture and execution.

sponsors. They must be "appropriate" companies. It would not do, for example, to receive sponsorship from a firm that exported leg irons or other instruments of captivity.

Some companies still see Amnesty as having political bias, being a left wing organization. It appears to them as a group of nameless people dealing with complex intellectual issues in far-away places and is unrelated to business. Since 1988, Amnesty has really been changing this kind of attitude. With careful publicity, it has drawn some of the world's most prominent businesses.

"Human Rights Now!"

The eighties and nineties have also been a time when the music world started taking notice of causes like Amnesty and the struggle for human rights. In 1988, the "Human Rights Now!" musical tour played massive concerts in stadia around the world – from Budapest to Brazil. The principal acts were Sting, Peter Gabriel, Bruce Springsteen, Youssou N'Dour and Tracy Chapman. The tour had a message for governments around the world and it sounded loud and clear: We Want Human Rights Now!

As Sting pointed out in an interview, rock stars are constantly asked to lend their name to this cause and that. Some of them, he complained, "can be rather vague and woolly, along the lines of 'Let's all hold hands and make the world a better place'. Somehow the logic of these events escapes me. When asked why I support Amnesty so strongly, I usually cite its focus on individuals."

On the night of September 6, 1988, the tour played its only show in the Eastern bloc: at Nepstadion in Budapest. It was an historic moment. Four days before the show, the Secretary General of Amnesty International, Ian Martin, was invited to Budapest by the United Nations Association there. He met representatives of the Hungarian government. It was the first time an Amnesty representative had met an official of an Eastern European government face to face, and

The sign of peace from a young demonstrator in Tiananmen Square, Beijing. On the night of June 3-4, 1989 and during the following days, over one thousand people were killed at a peaceful pro-democracy demonstration there. Heavily-armed troops opened fire on the crowd without warning. Students and spectators were shot at random. Men, women and children were crushed by tanks, beaten or shot as they tried to run away. This is the kind of repression Amnesty does not believe humanity has to put up with.

it was the start of Amnesty's missions there.

Behind the scenes at the Nepstadion, Janos Brody, a member of a sixties Hungarian rock band, Illes, was preparing for a surprise appearance on stage.

Brody's music had been banned in Hungary for comments he made in an interview after the Soviet invasion of Prague in 1968. On this night, twenty years later, he took the stage alone for a song called "If I Were a Rose", which he had written in 1973 about repression in the Eastern bloc. Although it had been banned and couldn't be broadcast at the time, this song had become familiar to everyone. It was "the hymn of the younger generation", as Brody put it.

Later that month, the "Human Rights Now!" tour reached North America. On September 17, they played to a near-capacity crowd of sixty thousand in the Olympic Stadium in Montreal, Canada. While Tracy Chapman was on stage, Sting was meeting a special group of women behind the scenes. These were Chilean refugees, relatives of the "disappeared", the same people Sting wrote his famous song, "They Dance Alone",

Sting on the "Human Rights Now!" tour. Bottom: The tour took in Europe, Asia, Africa and the Americas. By October 15, it had reached Buenos Aires.

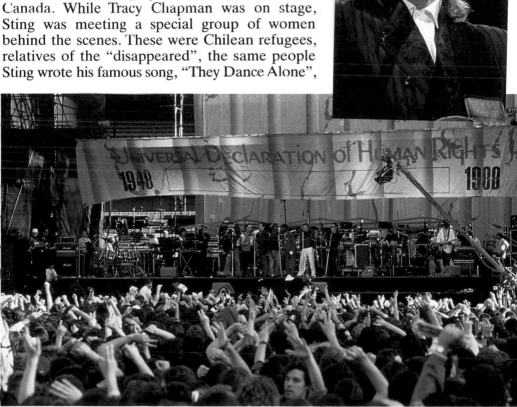

about. They wanted to thank him for publicizing their plight with the song. "I was so overwhelmed when I heard it," said Ximena Campos, whose brother Eduardo had disappeared in 1973. "I was so moved, I cried."

"Listen, Mr. Pinochet..."

In October 1990, two very special rock concerts took place in Chile. Everyone present was aware of one chilling fact: that the stadium where the concerts were taking place, Santiago's Olympic Stadium, had been a huge open air concentration camp during the rule of General Augusto Pinochet. Seventeen years before, thousands of people were tortured and imprisoned there. Many never left. There are still the bodies of some in the remaining sections of the walls.

On the nights of October 12 and 13, 1990, thousands gathered to hear famous rock stars. Peter Gabriel performed his famous song, "Biko", about Steve Biko, the South African Black Consciousness leader who died in mysterious circumstances while being interrogated by police. After the first word, the crowd began to roar. Traditional Chilean instruments provided a haunting backing. Then the stage filled with women dressed in black skirts and white tops carrying placards. They represented the mothers of all those who have "disappeared" in Chile – between 1,600 and 2,500 to date. The women, known as *Los Madres,* or Mothers, danced to Sting's song. They were dancing with their invisible fathers, brothers, and sons who are no longer with them.

"Listen, Mr. Pinochet," urged Sting, "don't buy any more weapons. Imagine your mother dancing alone."

"Thanks for remembering..."

On an even more impressive scale, "They Dance Alone" became something of an anthem in the campaign to defeat General Pinochet in Chile.

"Every city I've played in on my current tours, I've met los chileans," Sting said. "And each of them has said the same thing to me thanks for writing the song, ...for remembering what happened, thanks for telling the world what still happens in Chile."

The stars who made these concerts possible helped bring Amnesty's name to the ears of thousands of people, and by doing so, they

Sting dances with the mothers of missing Chileans. Such public exposure for the authorities in Chile can only cause them international embarrassment.

brought to light the stories of all prisoners of conscience the world over. New members flocked to join Amnesty – membership in Italy rose from eight thousand to twelve thousand almost overnight when Sting and Peter Gabriel appeared on a TV show there, talking about the forthcoming "Human Rights Now!" tour.

Keep the flame burning

1991 was Amnesty's thirtieth birthday. Like any anniversary, it prompted people to step back and look two ways: back into the past and forward into the future. It was a time to take hope from the achievements of Amnesty and to "refuel" enthusiasm to go on.

Also, as a birthday, it called for celebrations, and these happened all over the world. A huge crowd gathered outside St. Martin-in-the-Fields church in London and walked past Amnesty's first office, on May 28. In Belgium, the *Grote Markt* square in Brussels was filled with 529 lifesize cardboard silhouettes. Each one depicted the true story of a prisoner or missing person.

When it examined the world of 1991, Amnesty saw a time of sweeping changes, from the tumbling of walls in Eastern Europe to the crumbling of apartheid in South Africa. A particularly hopeful result of all this was the new sections Amnesty was able to open in countries to which they had previously only sent aid. At the International Council meeting of 1991, Amnesty welcomed with open arms new groups from Poland, Hungary, Algeria, Jordan, Macau, Malaysia and Taiwan. When Amnesty International was set up in 1961, the Cold War was at its peak. Late in 1990, a tiny new group in Moscow finally got underway a campaign for human rights. The Russian people were, at last, able to help to put things right in the world.

Amnesty International was celebrating thirty years of fighting for "forgotten" prisoners all over the world. As long as there is injustice, it will continue to do so.

"We will not have finished until cruelty, be it killing or torture, is seen as obscene and impermissible."

Peter Benenson, 1991.

Glossary

Allegation: An unproved statement or assertion, especially an accusation.

Amnesty: In everyday terms, a general pardon, especially for political offences. Amnesty International uses its influence to free all *prisoners of conscience;* ensure fair trials for political prisoners; abolish the death penalty, torture and other cruel treatment of prisoners; and end extrajudicial executions and "disappearances".

Bloc: A group of people or nations united by a common interest.

Capital crime: A crime that is punishable by death.

The Cold War: A state of hostility and military tension that existed between the USA and the Soviet *bloc* countries after World War II, involving propaganda, subversion, threats and other measures short of open warfare.

Commute: To change a punishment to one less severe. It is often used in terms of the death penalty.

Constitution: The fundamental political principles on which a state is governed.

Coup: Short for Coup d'Etat; a sudden violent or illegal seizure of government.

Delegate: A person chosen to represent others, especially at a conference or meeting.

Dossier: A collection of papers containing information on a particular subject or person.

Ethics: Social, religious or civil principles that are considered correct, especially those of a particular group, profession or individual.

Ideology: A body of ideas that reflects the beliefs and interests of a nation, or political system and underlies political action.

Inalienable: Not able to be transferred to another or taken away.

Indictment: A formal accusation of crime.

The Iron Curtain: The guarded border that existed between the countries of the Soviet *bloc* and the rest of Europe, also a non-physical barrier. The term was first used by Winston Churchill in 1956 and became part of the English language.

Legislation: The act of making laws.

Mandate: An instruction or set of instructions.

Political prisoner: Anyone imprisoned for holding, expressing, or acting according to political beliefs.

Posthumous: Occurring after death. Posthumous pardon, a pardon given after the person has been executed.

Prisoner of Conscience: Anyone imprisoned not for a crime but for their beliefs, race, sex, religion or ethnic origins.

Ratify: To agree with a formal signature.

Refugee: Someone who seeks shelter, usually in another country, from war, persecution or natural disaster.

Schizophrenic: A state of mind characterized by deterioration of the personality.

Statute: A permanent rule made by a body or institution for the government of its internal affairs.

Subversive: A person who works to overthrow a government illegally.

Terrorism: The use of terror, intimidation and violence to gain publicity for a cause and, usually, to achieve a political end.

Important Dates

1948   The United Nations adopts the Declaration of Human Rights.

1950: The European Convention on Human Rights is adopted by the Council of Europe.

1960: A British lawyer, Peter Benenson, reads an article about two Portuguese students who have been arrested and imprisoned for drinking a toast to liberty in a restaurant.

1961: "Appeal for Amnesty, 1961" is launched by Peter Benenson. Amnesty undertakes its first mission on behalf of a prisoner of conscience – to Czechoslovakia to appeal for the release of Archbishop Josef Beran. The first Amnesty group overseas is founded in West Germany, Holland, France, Italy and Switzerland follow.

1962: Amnesty International publishes its first newsletter. The cover features a Christmas card sent to a prisoner in Spain and returned marked "Consignee is free". Amnesty International deals with 210 cases in eleven countries.

1963: Amnesty comprises 350 groups.

1969: The American Convention on Human Rights – twenty countries from Central and South America ratify the convention.

1972: Amnesty International launches a worldwide campaign for the abolition of the use of torture.

1977: Amnesty International wins the Nobel Peace Prize.
Argentinian grandmothers set up *Abuelas de Plaza de Mayo* in an effort to locate their missing grandchildren.
Dec: In Stockholm, Amnesty holds a conference on the abolition of the death penalty.

1978: Amnesty International wins the United Nations Prize for Human Rights.

1979: The Arab Charter on Human Rights is drafted. Although discussed repeatedly throughout the 1980s, it is never fully adopted.

1983: Amnesty publishes its twelve point plan for the prevention of torture.

1985: Amnesty International's first educational pack entitled "Teaching and Learning about Human Rights" is distributed in British schools. Amnesty broadens its statute to include campaigns for refugees. There are 3,4330 groups in 55 countries, 200 more than the previous year, and over 500,000 members, supporters and subscribers.

1986: The African Charter on Human and Peoples' Rights come into force.

1987: A Genetic Data Bank is set up in Argentina.
Amnesty has 3,744 groups and sections in 44 countries.
The Philippines abolishes the death penalty.

1988: The "Human Rights Now!" tour plays concerts all over the world.

1989: Cambodia, Romania and New Zealand abolish the death penalty for all crimes against the state.

1990: Amnesty launches its Morocco campaign.
Ninety countries are now party to the International Covenant on Civil and Political Rights.

1991: Amnesty International celebrates its thirtieth anniversary.

1992: There are over 6,000 local Amnesty International groups in over 70 countries and over one million subscribers and donors in 160 countries, making it the largest human rights organization in the world.

Further Information

If you would like further information about the work of Amnesty International, or would like to become a member, contact their main office in your country.

International Secretariat
This is the central point for the planning of all Amnesty International's campaigns. It is here, also, that reports about human rights violations around the world are collected and published.

International Secretariat
Amnesty International,
1 Easton Street,
London WC1X 8DJ.

Australia
Amnesty International,
Private Bag 23,
Broadway,
Sydney South,
New South Wales 2007.

Canada
[English-speaking]
Amnesty International,
130 Slater Street, Suite 900,
Ottawa,
Ontario K1P 6E2.

[French-speaking]
Amnistie Internationale,
6250 boulevard Monk,
Montreal,
Quebec H4E 3H7.

Ireland, Republic of
Amnesty International,
Sean MacBride House,
8 Shaw Street,
Dublin 2.

New Zealand
Amnesty International,
PO Box 793
Wellington 1.

United Kingdom
Amnesty International,
99-119 Rosebery Avenue,
London EC1R 4RE.

United States of America
Amnesty International of the USA,
322 8th Ave,
New York,
NY 10001.

Index